After Modigliani

Also by Stephen Kessler

AFTER MODIGLIANI

poems

Stephen Kessler

CREATIVE ARTS BOOK COMPANY
Berkeley • 2000

Many of these poems first appeared, in one form or another, in the following publications, whose editors are gratefully acknowledged: *The Bardian, Cedar Hill Review, Chiron Review, Dallas Review, Exquisite Corpse, The Gab, Green Fuse, Hambone, Luna, Mama Yama, The Mendonesian, The Montserrat Review, New Delta Review, North Bay Gardens, Outlook, Oxygen, Quicksilver, Rain City Review, Sheila-Na-Gig, The Steelhead Special, This Is Important, Volt;* and in *A Flame in the Heart: A Love/Hate Anthology* (Littoral Press) and *The Geography of Home: California's Poetry of Place* (Heyday Books).

After Modigliani is published by Donald S. Ellis and distributed by Creative Arts Book Company

For information contact:
Creative Arts Book Company
833 Bancroft Way
Berkeley, California 94710

For ordering information call:
1-800-848-7789
Fax: 1-510-848-4844

Graphics and Book Design by Pope Graphic Arts Center
Cover Art: Giraudon / Art Resource, NY
Modigliani, Amedeo (1884-1920)
Nu a la chemise, 1918.

ISBN 0-88739-265-2
Library of Congress Catalog Number 99-61371

Printed in the United States of America

Contents

After Modigliani

Second Language

To touch, in this tongue, is to play, as in:
I touch the keys of the machine and music emerges,

or: He plays the piano's hammers and out bounce sounds
of utmost harmonic meanings, cables through which

messages move at the speed of blood
and undone hair as it rumbles

over shoulders and under doors into gutters where flows
every stray stroke of what the city wastes:

melodies far too far removed to
rescue memory, touches, the tart

cruelties, those old kisses and intimate
whispers too numerous to recount and too hard

to prove except for the aching evidence now
turned furtive, safely flirtatious, playful, touchingly

attuned to rhythmic polyphony of fingers whose movements
feint or intimate further movement toward the beautiful

April City

You can tell it's spring
by the smell of diesel fumes
floating up to the fifth floor
from where they're fixing the street
and the soot hangs like a halo
of lights illuminating a stadium
over the city drifting into open windows
and settling like a black snowdrift on the desk

machinery grinds day and night
and across the river the jets
swoop into Newark or scream for Europe overhead
the trees are exploding green
obscuring the stark view through their beautiful
bare branches all winter long that I loved
and the nights are warm enough to walk
naked into and not be noticed

High Holy Day

Why does that rusty Mercury spattered with guano
parked by Mike's Papaya
seem to be scowling on such a splendid afternoon.
The car alarms warble happily
along with the whoops of the fire trucks
as they cruise for arsonists on Yom Kippur,
the city festive in its endless
atonement-free incendiary excess,
the woman rioting in the post office line
a natural companion to the man who drools
unconscious in the subway car, his cardboard sign
explaining his condition
lettered on the back of a joy-of-smoking ad
illegibly wedged against the plastic seat.
My stranger in the stained sweatshirt pleads for change
I can't afford to contribute—
I'm saving up for taxi fare
whenever I can get away.
All these fathers and mothers strolling their babies
rebuke my mood with their grins.
The sun seems kind even as it fries
its fine mutations into our helpless cells.
A picture of Charlie Manson on the t-shirt of a jogger
turns out as he approaches
to be Shakespeare—
authors of tragedies, tawdry has-beens,
immortal sources of blood and publicity.
No honors for those who refuse to sleep
with roaches in the glow of the refrigerator light,
no peace for daughters of divorce
from the rage of the uncontrollable telephones.
Three teenage girls on the corner of Broadway
decline to do business with the wandering merchant

hawking his broken suitcase full of Victoria's Secret catalogs
and expired subscriptions to *Life*
and headsets disconnected from everything.
Runners in packs cut swift paths
through the park's green shade, religious, fit,
more blessed than the woman in the token booth
or crack-addled Karen in her sidewalk office
hustling passersby. The thing is
to seek music, I suppose,
squeeze some trace of sweetness
out of this inexplicably bitter hour. But look,
the cheerful dogs are romping leashless
in the weakening light, the highway is humming with speed,
a skater blading day-glo circles backward between the benches.
What makes their grace
so difficult for me.

Tobacco

I like the taste of tobacco.
Most cigarettes stink, but to smoke
an after-dinner hand-rolled Drum
or to puff on a Dutch or Caribbean cigar
on a fall morning with the windows open
is one of the simpler gifts of civilization.
Tobacco is a vice
not just because it can kill you
but because the pleasure of its flavor
recurrently seduces—
like exercise or sex
or the impulse to turn
and gaze at gorgeous women going by.
That grace of motion, that sensory bath
is like the intoxicating haze
of swirling smoke that surrounds you
as you exhale the aromatic clouds
of contentment, a bittersweet aftertaste
lingering on your tongue.
It is redolent of the den
in my childhood home
where Sunday mornings in October
my father would watch football
and smoke and schmooze with his friends,
my brothers, me, all men
gathered in a flickering ritual
of athletic imagination
while the smells of bacon and French toast and coffee
hung around for hours after breakfast
mixing amiably with the darker essence of long Havana cigars.
When I smoke I am recycling those smells
and associations, resurrecting the old man,
seasoning my bloodstream with his cured aura,

inoculating my nose against any foul insult
the sidewalk offers
or the years may try to impose.
As I draw smoke I draw strength,
invoke ghosts, think of Lin Yutang
savoring his pipe, meditate emptily
absorbing the leaves glittering
play of shadows on the littered ground.
I can summon the echo of a conversation
with an old friend in California,
breathe the corrupted breeze of this New York park
as if it were the clear air of Oregon.

So Long Miles

Silver rivulets of musical light
streak through the sky over East St. Louis
as Miles rises like a bright moon
into an immortality of weird sweet bitter
winding
                soaring
                                gliding
swooping notes impossible to play
but someone's blowing them
                                creating
noises unheard before
in communion with a wild
tight band of collaborators
                                conspiring to explore
space & time
                scientists of the spirit
                                                out there
like astronauts
                        like stars and steel
rails gleaming in the great night
                                                miles
and miles across unhealable America
a stream of soothing and disturbing rhythms
that bathe the organism in orgasms of grace
and wring this grief of gratitude for your gone
life, Miles,
                the yellowjackets echoing your cool style
armed with a sharp
                        soft hard barbed
                                                sound
able to sting repeatedly and not retreat
but live on to sing and wound again
                                                effortlessly
raising the stakes

for everyone
                                    setting original standards
of endurance amid the relentless stresses

standards of transformation

_____

Now out of your voice
come the daily sirens
with their lights of burning blood
revolving
                    the lovers' low tones
late at night
                         when bottles are smashed
against stone stairs
and subway trains are crushing the air
asleep in tunnels underground
                                              your guerrilla sound
always alive to surprise even the rats
who scat in the streets and dance
                                        drugged
on the music of your memory
                                    sunset
Spanish-tinged as in rouged and flashing-black-eyed Flamenco
farewells above the skyline of Hoboken
                                                    cities pulsing
in the stream lines of your inconsolable cries
all tears
              mingling with yours
                                        all blues blending
into your pure undertow
                                    all tender lips
kissing the edge of your blade
a slide shining
                         always with ageless faces
laughter given over to a slippery gravity

8

on morning playgrounds
                        fameless and neverending

———————————————

Every breath is instrumental
every silence like a stolen radio
forcing the violated to listen
                        inspired
to the whole hurricane of crime
                        and pain
devastating the city
emergency room music to treat the wounded
scales of severity to transfuse
the uncool
            the beautiful
                        as they board buses
inhaling ruinous fumes
                        and the river runs upstream
mimicking your contrary currents
                        your spatial
contradictions
            your distinct lyric dissonances
dredged up from the deep
                        with difficult ease
more perfectly arced than any basketball
falling touchless at the buzzer for the victorious
score

Miles, the game is yours
we are merely amazed witnesses
dismembered listening
                        blessed and electrified
by precise lightning
                        long streaks that hang in the sky
unchained

Great Divide Crossing

Your window exposes visions of the city
spilling into the river, sludgelike rush hour
pierced by shrieks of ambulance blood
flashing toward some ordinary affliction.

Across the street by the park,
five stories down, adjacent to the playground,
a taxi pulls over, the driver gets out
and relieves himself on a tree.

Pissing distance from the front steps
a junked sofa rests in the bushes,
living room for the roofless—abused smokers
who also suck the exhaust of the M5.

Each bus is an island of light
in the deepening dusk,
faces in windows reflecting
on the day's violations.

A kind moment—a hand given
to an old woman losing her balance
as the bus lurched—stays in a girl's mind
as she rides home with her mother.

A barge is towed upriver by a tug,
and beyond, the concrete honeycombs,
purple light behind Hoboken,
Pennsylvania farmland, coal country, the plains.

I was carried across the Rockies, the desert,
the Sierras in a jet
and touched down in the dry heat
of a May afternoon.

Entering the green, past the dead depot
amid the commercial parking lots of Petaluma,
I breathed all the reasons I need:
spring grasses and the breeze over Point Reyes.

Even the crushed skunks
and log trucks of Mendocino littering the road
with shreds of redwood corpses and
spewing their smoke in tourists' faces

only accentuate the grace of waves,
ospreys, toppled grandfathers
crashing into the brush
with thunderous thuds.

A man with a chainsaw
carves stumps into sculpture
in his front yard; a young woman
flirts with three guys in front of a store.

Small trees are putting out fruits
like little green baseballs,
soon to be edible,
summer's juices running;

strawberries sweeten
on their leafy mounds
and slender seedlings
take strength from the sun.

Eucalyptus Love Call

Hundreds of miles of wild eucalyptus
litter the state with their excessive flesh,
shedding it in long strips to reveal the smooth white limbs
you want to stroke as you speed past.

True, the trees are as fiction
to the competing reality of rental cars
and movie marquees pressing their positions
on the city, marketplace of homicide stories
and disappearances that don't go away—

a faded land whose sky you
choke on, nostalgically invoking
a simpler time that didn't exist
but once, a moment of exploding magnolias
and streetcars where when you reached out the window
you slashed your hand on the fast foliage.

The trees took over, transplanted from some distant South,
shaking their manes like ghosts of gorgeous hippies
believing what couldn't be—
free love spreading its seeds, everything given,
given away, a revolution in beauty.

Walt Whitman casts his gaze over the coast
and down the road to that great thick grove
posted against trespassers
where he and I have hung out at length,
leaning back high on the spicy smell,
our longing wandering among the slim trunks
that reach up, up.

I want to strip away layers,
a gesture of surrender;
abandon the battle
in favor of embraces.

I tend to a slender eucalypt,
caressing its trunk as it takes a foothold.
Yet it grows stronger if you leave it be.

Bobcat

Standing on Tek's back deck at dusk
I met a bobcat coming into the clearing
to hunt rabbits in the brush.

He stopped when I spoke to him,
watched me watching him—
or maybe he was a she—

a bobcat anyhow, that far away,
stalking his prey
but distracted.

Tek and I were on our way
to eat at the Golden Buddha,
a restaurant he'd avoided.

Can you imagine, he asked, the Golden
Virgin Mary? The Golden Jesus?
I thought of the golden calf,

the golden cat.
We couldn't leave the deck
while he held our gaze.

My first bobcat, Tek said.
I'd seen one once, but running,
at night, in headlights, not this close.

We watched the cat
and the cat watched us,
forgetting about dinner.

Time slowed, expanded. Then
he turned, slinked off into the brush,
short tail flicking so-long.

We drove down Tola Ranch Road
toward town, pleased
to share this world

with such a creature. Suddenly
the cat sprang out of the brush,
crossed the road in front of us

for luck.

Why I Haven't Called

I am winked at nightly by a flirtatious lighthouse.
I have an erection for the whole horizon,
desire to hold and breathe its rolling flora,
admire its changing sky, sunset
spreading its fetching blush
like rouge on a feminist.

My vision is imprinted with aftershocks of your face
as we mated, you let me adore your beauty,
inhabiting you, being your body,
our hearts smashing into each other
like surf and rocks,
merciless as electricity.

Illumination. Mountains trembling.
Who gasps last when the orgasms are over.
Who lives on with clear mind
amid the crime waves clobbering all architecture.

My glasses are dusty with disasters, gangsters.
Having that automatic aimed at me had consequences.
Shinran Shonin saw the whole thing,
just as he witnessed Fat Man fall on Hiroshima.
Ever since then I see my life
flashing through me all day like an X ray,
flesh transparent, image of its brevity to the bones,
spirit escaping, no more nights with you.

How can I cast doubt on our casting couch.
Our story is indisputable,
lodged in the canon like a loaded shell
inside whose explosive charge you hear the ocean,
sounds of owls' wings and refrigerators,

see the satanic tankers, tugs on the smelly Hudson,
kestrels hovering and shooting into meadows for mice,
see us clashing, reconciling in spirals,
postmasters issuing special stamps commemorating our passion.

Last night I dreamed I lost you in a crowd,
some kind of coliseum, a one-time appearance
by a certain soloist
or speech by a famous thinker.
We were separated by a sea of heads.

Sacred Space

A minute to midnight Easter Sunday
and he is risen, high on the diary of Anne Frank,
dinner with the new neighbors, half a joint,
Miles Davis and two Bohemias.
The light is mothlike,
scattering its radiant dust over every object
and subject in sight, pages of blank absences
and bright young eyes alive to doom and unblinking,
embracing fate like a first love and dying into it
with huge grief, unspeakable.

Night.

Yet also alchemical feats of wild survival.
The words walking away from the author
like handsome children growing into lives
only they can imagine. Keeping her voice
more real than history, a strong sweet light
in the deepening planetary disaster,
proof that enthusiasm is possible
even when your family is condemned.

How even to speak to you from this far.
You make me cry as if I'd lost a lover,
grateful for the gift
and destroyed at the same time.

Jesus never did this,
never tore into me like a contemporary—
gangbanger brother of a poet I know
gunned down in East L.A.
or Manhattan crack addict panicky in the subway
trying to sell me a TV.

I would have joined some family
but my mind was too much my own.
I was new, shy, like you,
smart in the worst way, self-aware,
doubly present
inwardly and out.

I had to come home
and record the lost moth
rattling in the Japanese lamp.

The Possessed

Silence illumines the new afternoon
pale sun seeping thru beige haze

in what should be summer but is cool
like self-possessed lovers

sharing a brew in public
passionate thirsts contained

wild weather
all those homeless storms

the first sighs of surrender and relief
when survivors celebrate their arrival

along the smooth clean skin the tongue explores
tentatively tasting the sweet buds of sensation

nipples attentive to the new pleasure
every firm curve alert yet langorous

all the horizontal afternoon
smelling of eucalyptus and bougainvillea

slender wires draped over the street
conducting electric languages

What Are You Doing

The city's so huge you could be anywhere
calling strange men to look at their furniture
interviewing thugs for a scoop
dancing in a club with your escort service
or listening to me on your machine
as you laugh over my skillet with your dinner guest

it used to be that when the flames sang
your heat was with me
as in those evenings
putting our paper to bed
above the small-town street
fluorescent light of the production room
flickering discreetly with our secret

the earthquake saved us
fused our fragments
drove us whole into the broken world
all our comings are recorded always
in the libraries of our cells

but tonight all I can remember is
you haven't returned my call

Vegan Tart

Her contradictions are seductive to me
the leather miniskirt & plastic platform pumps
the foul mouth delicately enveloping
steamed greens & brown rice
her taste in poets running to Dickinson & Bukowski
she smokes handrolled tobacco only
drives a 5-speed admires flowers & hates dogs
on summer nights she lies down on the deck
naming the constellations & giving out little gasps
when a satellite or meteor unexpectedly transgresses
she smells like fresh-cut weeds after a wet winter
green light brightening her brain
like the space above the pool table in a dark bar
every thought brilliantly afloat & glittering
over a game of colorful & subtle collisions
percussion of ivory kissing
her teeth tough enough to bite thru barbwire
behind unspeakably tender & expressive lips

Madonna Unmasked

Why were you so kind to me
in my sleep
your makeup had melted
revealing a woman
warmer than the myth

you regarded me as a comrade
a brother in tenderness
we went out arm in arm
and the consumers
admired us from a distance
leaving us alone
to enjoy oneness

we were like friends
who after many years
understand each other unspoken
who understate their love
as if to acknowledge aloud
their intimacy in its depth
would be indecent

instead they joke
trade gossip and commentary
confessing their affection
only as an aside

harmony the musicians call it
the audience unaware
the hours days whole lives
of exercise
working on the fit for their few notes
watching each other's eyes

so in the dream this pleasure
flooded my consciousness with calm
a sense nothing could go wrong
as long as our alliance lasted
irony and desire the great antidotes

all else incidental
to the undoing of our distances

Anecdotal Evidence

A summer day at last
and in the mild evening
after the dishes are washed and dripping
a spider races out from under a sponge
the house perfumed with garlic
and a sweet breeze swimming through the windowscreen

heat relieves something
and releases some other longing
seasonal associations only
the smell of someone's skin
glazed lightly with sweat
on a bed in the afternoon
green light glittering through Sunday trees

anecdotal evidence
honorable mention in retrospect
as new tasks are assumed
indoor insects to rescue and remove
a treatise to compose on the cult of potency
a bucket of compost to dump and turn
a Drum to roll and smoke on the deck after dinner
thin clouds pinkening beyond a looping bat

small details of an unremarkable day
whose beauty might go otherwise unremarked
and whose little elusive mysteries and illuminations
brighten the mind toward midnight

Sleeping in Shelley's Ashes

I slept on the beach where Shelley drowned
and was burned right there by his friends
it was 1966 and we were driving up from Rome
and there were no vacancies in Viareggio
so Dave Mann drove his red VW bug onto the beach
and got stuck in the sand and we spread our pink plastic
laundry sacks from the laundromat in Venice
and lay there under the Mediterranean sky
gawking up at the summer stars and freezing
and being eaten by insects and I could feel
the zits on my unbathed back erupting with pus
on one of the most romantic nights of my life
which may explain why I became a poet
because I passed that first initiative ordeal
and went on to endure far greater discomforts
in the pursuit of rooms for rent and elusive muses
sleeping in Shelley's ashes was essential
I relish the smell of his charred but fireproof heart
even tonight under a cool California sky
whose stars are veiled by coastal mist
and whose thin moon has set hours since
just past dusk in this other summer

This Magic Moment

Was it Clyde McPhatter
who solo'd on that song
in 1959 when I was 12
and would soon be learning to cruise
directionless but for the discovering ride
through night streets with no shortcuts
but the city's discrete details
dialed into the psyche
with waves of contagious music
that had us dancing

as if it were the midnight
stroke of some major holiday
the holy men getting nailed
or coming back from the dead
or crossing the desert kvetching
or sailing over to a new world and getting lost
or perhaps the uprising of the enslaved patriarchs
or just another year
turning around on schedule like the lamb
on the gyro spit at Jerusalem felafel

something to celebrate
because fire is alive and so is wine
and we are here to witness miracles
thriving in the face of their fierce heat
satellites conspiring like billiard tables
to bank back into the receiving jaw
some brilliant echo of revelation

yes it's true I am a one-man cult
master of nothing but my own ceremonies
imagining the all-powerful

impact of doo-wop
on my inflammatory cache of incantations
illegal weapons of a private religion

Ben E. King is the correct cantor
and the time is 1960
eternal flames confirm these facts
and so the Drifters rise and serenade
the sun as it comes up

The New Politics

So you are fumigating a smoke-filled room
with bittersweet reflections that curl toward the open window
as wild animals pillage the cat food
and die of hypertension before your eyes

it is the year of the crushed raccoon
year of the suitcase packed and unpacked
and repacked as you moved roofless
between homes like an actor between bad films
year of the hammer and the smashed thumb

you've seen it all and you can't get enough
afraid to stare at the face across
and leering anyway because you can't help yourself
you need the first woman's help
as she sweeps the incumbent dust
and it comes back to glaze the surfaces
faithfully as a tongue on love's long torso

hold us close as we come you cry
like a hit song thru a car radio
causing the driver to writhe
you haven't felt so alive
since the space shuttle exploded
or before when wives obeyed
and wild men roamed the streets in shredded pants
begging bystanders for meat money

that dust in your eyes is tears
that food in your beard is drugs
you were informed on and made to spell out loud
your mother's maiden name to prove you were born

but nothing helped
the channels kept changing
and now it is the year of the magazine cover
leaping from the shopping cart to catch your look
in the checkout line

it is the year of laughter and fasting
year of aerobic grandmothers
toting Kalashnikovs to the Capitol
mad as panthers from California
in the last hours of empire

Weather Report

An adversarial January
storm after storm after storm
attacking all things trying to drive
or stay home without stovepipes backing up
and smoke suffocating inspiration

24 years to the day
since I married the girl of my nightmares
Nixon's ghost floats in the overhead light
three nights since I held my nemesis
her urbane embrace civilizing the wildman
and tomorrow at noon a new president
instating his own cutthroats
in place of the previous thieves
lately making off with the law

your voice got modemed into an alien line
nothing but raspy static on the underwater cable
whisper louder muse or whoever you are
the fax isn't coming through

when Cocteau's ambulance overtook us
we had no idea it was headed for our house
but it got lost
divided as we are
our beds miles apart across slides
flash floods the jaws of life and slick
steep streets up which some cars can't
swim

the roads are blind with ambition
to get someplace against the blinding downpours
a tired seeing-eye dog

takes its place at the hearing table
answers questions like a cabinet minister
sniffing the wind
obedient under its soaked fur
for sale as a wrap to the coldest socialite

Dr. Frankenstein throws the switch
to catch the life-giving lightning
but no dice
the monster dozes as the sky beats down
and the doctor cries out loud like Hopkins in the dark
and is mistaken for Lon Chaney under a full moon
and shot at from a small plane
which makes a crashing sound
along the coast

it's only waves bark the cove dwellers
safe in the comfort of their mobilehomes
the campground floating uphill at high tide
the stationer's envelopes' damp flaps
stuck shut
the dump a swamp
games rained out despite the teams' great love of mud

horns can be heard
car horns executive tenors
dizzy brass handlebars on which the dying ride
strokes of genius guide the brush into old age
trailing childish watercolors

Jack's Last Words

That last afternoon
when the nurse came in
and sucked the liquid out of his lungs
with a plastic tube down his nose
plugged in the wall
my father said
when she was done
"Give her a dollar"

he always was the big tipper
maybe because his sister
when their old man didn't come home
had to quit school and take a job as a waitress
he knew it was tough to work
and so he tipped

he barely spoke that day
the sun of L.A. blazing mid-July
cool room shady
facing the Hollywood Hills
Hamburger Hamlet across the street
where we ate
waiting for him to die

each of us had our turn
to be with him alone
lying there dignified
silent in the white sheets
face hollowed out and bald head glowing
radiation tanned
I told him he looked beautiful
and he groaned
the bandage around the i.v.
was too tight

after the nurse fixed that
he had a couple of hours
I was there for a while
the two of us just quiet
until he said with a shrug
in his tired voice
"I paid for it"

Marty's Mother

She wanted her ashes scattered
at Dodger Stadium
every time someone slides into third base
a puff of her dust
would float toward the floodlights

Vivian's voice had a tough
but affectionate edge
sweetened by watching Maury Wills
beat out cheap hits in 1962
and who knows what Yiddish history
absorbed in her Brooklyn youth

when we were kids
and we came over
she said as we left
"It was nice having had you"

years later
Maury got popped for coke
and Marty became a shrink
and I whom it was nice having had
a poet and former infielder
small but slow
with a nose for form
and no arm

Vivian it's been 30 years
missing you isn't the issue
but I want for a moment to go back
with your boy
to the real grass of our adolescence
secretly seeding at 2 a.m.
your memory in the gameless dark

Larry Hart

Why am I thinking of Larry Hart
boyhood playmate I wrestled with
later to be my rival
handsome varsity athlete
track star punter and wide receiver
driver of the coolest midnight blue '57 Chevy coupe
which drove me hopeless with jealousy
when I'd cruise by the home of Helen McCann on Elm
and see it parked on the street
knowing he was inside
going long

eleven years later Larry appeared
at our first high-school reunion
prematurely middle-aged at 28
his beautiful body gone to banker's fat
sinewy swiftness over the high hurdles
less than a memory
young stud's radiance a legendary fiction
Helen long since married and divorced
and teaching elementary school at Horace Mann

even the Chevy retired to some yard
a rusting carcass
picked over for parts

Saturday

Pitching the old rolled roofing
with its pitchy underside
from the back of the pickup
into the bottomless pit of the Fish Rock dump
I smelled the stench of the rotting residue
of the whole region's leftovers
which cut thru the crisp wind like sickness itself

oxygen intervened
the trees breathing
what strength remained
before the arrival of the last chainsaw
and the torn seam of my glove's thumb
permitting a little filth or fertility
to feel my skin

a bright day
downtown such as it was
with no stoplights and the ocean
breaking on Main Street
alive with visitors like gulls
circling the dump's immense mounds
or ravens cruising a carcass
crushed in the road

a bright day sliced with black wings
even as breath comes
somehow
feeding the blood

Year of the Rat

Those little nests of soft debris
wedged in the hollows of the woodpile
and the perfectly formed pellets
like tiny dry footballs
scattered lightly on this or that piece
of split dried oak under the tarp

are evidence of their presence
but despite the fever
they're said to have smuggled up from the Southwest
the thought of their snouts and sharp teeth and long
hard tails all of which remain
discreetly hidden from my gloved hand
as it unstacks firewood to warm the house

is nowhere near so worrisome as
the feral families near the subway rails
undaunted by screeching trains
or ducking into a gap
in the stone stairs of the park
or gnawing on pizza by the garbage cans
five stories down or who knows smoking crack
inside some abandoned mattress across the street

or maybe most frightening of all one midnight
darting out of a lot right under our feet
while we strode up Sixth Avenue as if
the city belonged to us and not the rats

Nature Is Hell

How can you be a Taoist
& use a power trimmer to whack the grass

what grows is shredded or pulled or paved
& keeps coming back anyway

why such effort to suppress the primal
nightmare of vines & slime

what homestead didn't have to be hacked out
what garden never died or was devoured

each night deer conspire
raccoons trespass to scavenge

snails gophers carpenter ants & the diabolical
diabrotica maraud

see those green shoots drive their blades
right through the eye

nature is hell

yet those clouds out there
at sundown are something else

Cigarette Case

When you come to smoke
with me in the mountains
I like the spark in your eyes
when we light up

the mist over the river reminds me
of the drift our friendship follows
through years of dinners in town
at Chinese restaurants where the beer
in our frosted mugs cooled and seduced
our tongues as we talked

in the pavilion of moonlit religion
tobacco was our sacrament
and the taste of gossip
left us reckless
with useless and beautiful
bad habits

At Buk's in Fort Bragg

Nine days after your death
I'm with my date, a poet,
in this saloon we figure
must be named for you.
The bartender passes out
condoms in a plastic basket
and the other patrons,
three guys and a woman,
are talking loud about the size
of dicks they've known.
Smoke from the mill
a few blocks west
smears the night sky white.
I hear the words "Charles"
and "dog from hell" and know
we're in the right place,
a dive in the tradition.
My friend brags of crashing
the boys' pool table
at some artists' colony you
would have shunned like sobriety,
and asks me if I shoot pool
and I shrug, sure.
Three quarters
and a game of 8-ball later
she thinks I've hustled her,
not understanding modesty
is different from deception.
We've had a few drinks tonight
and we feel close, intimate
enough for her to scoop
a few free condoms from the basket
just in case. She says she feels

too weird to consummate
our sweet allegiance
in an act of love,
wants only to go home
and write a poem
together in your memory.
The table's green light
glows like fire
as the barflies
laugh us out the door.

The Marlon Brando Diet

My ice cream binges are history; from here on
all I consume are tacos al pastor
and carrot juice, cruising used-book stores

for copies of my memoirs, which I lift
into my large pockets and carry lightly
into the street, layers of ancient fat

confusing the security machines
as I dance past, shedding pounds
like the contender I could have been.

Women I once seduced with a few grunts
look younger now and pass me without a glance,
hooked into headsets pumping them full

of the newest excuse for music, my lost looks
spread too thin over too many used years
to pull their magnetic chemistry toward mine,

too thick and rich to get their arms around.
And yet, see how my radius recedes,
memory's excess burned away by grief.

Strangers in a Strange Night

What was the name of that dive near the beach on Seabright
the one with the pool table & the nautical motif
where F.A. & I went to have a few beers one night
something like 20 years ago at least

we must have shot a couple of rounds of 8-ball
& dropped a few more quarters into the jukebox
while flirting from a distance with the lone woman
drinking at the far end of the bar

F.A. was the one who struck up a conversation
I was too shy to deploy that kind of charm
but it happened her place was right around the corner
just in back of the lit-up laundromat

so she invited us over & into her bed
all three of us throwing our clothes on the studio floor
& groping thru the beer & nothingness
for some warm animalistic consolation

in my fastidiousness I fucked her first
I couldn't have stood to shove it in F.A.'s mess
& as he fucked her I put my hand on his back
in some kind of brotherly lover's solidarity

& after he came & rolled off there was a pause
the three of us once more quietly on our own
names forgotten bodies released for a moment
till she said with a casual gesture "There's the door"

Safe Sex

The only sex that's safe is poetry.
Intercourse of eyes is a distant second.
Third, kissing in a stolen car
parked under a streetlamp on a cliff.
From there it's a steep drop
into deep danger.

We know how ridiculous desire is,
what idiots we are under its influence,
but to move in unison
toward oneness—
the whole dark
drawing us in, as in art

the act raising us out of ourselves
into rapids sweeping us downriver,
pulling us to the mouth where sweet
mixes with salt and the waters'
bodies are ambiguous, nameless, mutually
absorbed and dissolving.

Know how far apart we are
and weep, it's a relief, the closest thing
to climax we have,
grief rising to the eyes
and spilling on pages we wish were lips
savoring the aloneness of our own.

Phantom Self-Portrait in a Wall Collage

The face in the mirror
in the photograph is "hers," obscurely

backlit and beshadowed doubly
from behind the balcony's glass

door, spookily beautiful and strange
beyond reach like a distant intimate

unrecoverable recollection stuck
in the midst of many other irreconcilable

images. I resemble the condemned
moviehouse on Main Street

nowhere in sight, the dead screen echoing
absentee stars and stories never to be

seen again, invisible ripples spreading
economically through every business on the

empty block, customers suddenly missing
minus the necessary narratives, and I

among them reading mail instead
including what never arrived:

one thank-you note, one IOU, one
argument over fidelity

in translation, one clipping
concerning the phantom's fame, and one

request for money—all of a piece
with my current drugless discipline

of study and exercise, jealous sexual
fantasies fed by no phone calls, fear

that face may never appear again
except in reruns kept in a red box

in a drawer I dread opening
for its threatening obsession—

oldest song in the book, over-
recorded by every chanteuse

in Los Angeles. Whatever became
of that script which made us rich?

Checkout Time

After we finish lunch at the Sizzling Tandoor
where the Russian River crosses Highway 1
let's say we go to a motel in Bodega Bay
and celebrate our separation
recollecting as at year's end
or the approach of the millennium
every heroic moment of our history
feeling tasting smelling the unique contours
of our changing collaboration

let us acknowledge again the sacrament
we shared in the religion we performed
review the record of our arguments
and determine who is the loser after all
recall every woman on the New York streets
who turned my abandoned look from you
and total up the checks and balances
rising and falling with our blessed bodies
stormtides tossing up lost evidence
of lives we forgot we had
long nights alongside the glittering river
Andalusian trains in search of a warm room
dinner breaks on deadline night
going over to your place for a nap
parties with the flirtatious governor
the charming chancellor the candidates
all in the name of news which was our love

how did it start and what really happened
we'll have all afternoon to figure it out
and evening too and night if necessary
it could take years to get the story straight
we'll have to hire a scribe to write it down

in verse so it'll be easier to remember
when the beautiful children we never had
initiate their own kids in the legend
all the savory details flowing like saliva
between our competing complementary tongues

come with me someplace where we can talk
like friends who may not see each other again
and want to be sure they've settled with the desk
and left the key and taken everything

Variations on the Greek

1

You lie entwined with your latest man
a beautiful youth your age whose smooth
mind you may use as you please and whose
skin you fuse with easily as you fuck

2

Every night you lay with a new lover
I suffered remembering what they felt
as they moved through the long pleasure
of your bones the power of your athlete
muscle tone and the high silent sweetness
of your shuddering release

3

With each fresh man
my agony increased
until the misery was obliterated

Black Box

What useless cruelties we waste on each other, crimes
of passion and painful cuts inflicted with wits too fine

for their own enlightenment, as if to butcher
the acres of beds we blessed together perfecting

our legendary duet, photos recording what passes
through us like fresh steel every time we look, your

birthday at the Boardwalk, our sex-relaxed forms reflected
in the jewelry-shop window—DIAMONDS, GOLD—or just
   implacably

imprinted in recollection like New York nights and our hot
fights in the street unlike anything else felt,

that terrible intensity, so much emotion smoked up
fast like crack, six years richer at the lost end

of incredible highs under the influence of books
we almost got around to reading before the library

was divided. This is my final spiral into the sea
like a fighter pilot corkscrewing toward oblivion, dizzy

in the cockpit, your picture stuck on the control panel
speaking your last lines too, sharply, sick of how long

it's taken to be done with the death of tenderness, an endless
parting kiss whose tongues mysteriously froze or

melted us together, fused into a soul whose true
allegiances were twisted in the effort to separate. The bodies

split and adhere elsewhere, drifting to milder
psyches than those who cause the surprise rage out of which

jam jars are thrown at slamming doors and uncomprehended
letters received with the eloquence of explosives, wounding

whoever opens. How purely the rhythms of our songs, our art
forever affixed to the walls witnessed and accompanied the

casualties, the pleasures too infinite to believe, even now
intimate with a sinking moon I can almost still feel how

your cervix sweetened the hundred-year flood of my gratitude,
think of an afternoon nap or Sunday newspaper morning when

we poured our syrup in praise and tasted every
loneliness destroyed, exactly what now we must re-create

each in discrete distortion of the ephemeral
history we wrote for the front page, inside

pages, dedication pages, pages flying from typewriters
and printers that spit their texts on the office floor

where the boss with luck may slip and be liquidated,
the face we mirrored undermined, buried in rockslides

of hard words. Invective is not avalanche enough
to level or resurrect what endures, the evidence exists

though murdered, it lives in the eyes that contact
you lovingly nevertheless who knows why even as your gaze

engages its own image reflected in a tear-streaked screen

Confession of No Faith

The ink is fading on the famous letters.
Old men's photos fade in their frames
even as their words keep squirming.
I hear the mineral water rebelling
in its French jelly jar,
slowly going flat like the Big Bang.
My hammer hangs in the pantry
like an old pen I stopped writing poems with
because words went soft, gave up pretending
to nail the impossible and just lay there
like disappearing ink in a framed
document on the wall, all the genius
in the wrist that wrote it gone
nobody knows where.
They all did the same thing—died—
and so will I
and we let fly anyway
ridiculous wind-driven squawks.
I want to cry but I can't,
not even a shrink could squeeze
tears out of me now, that stream
is dammed, I don't know why.
I want to recover the old men
but it's like going into the undertow,
you're in it too, there's nothing to save,
no rescue outside time,
moments you have one chance each
to touch as they're sucked away. I'm twisted
over the one with the smell I worship
who wishes me invisible, the one
who thinks I'm the competition,
the one who wants me to keep cool
while she settles accounts

with her other men, the one who brings out
the philosopher in me with her radiant face.
I don't know how to be decent, obedient,
how to proceed. So I confess
like an apologist
for a faith I lack—
some guy rising from the grave, give me a break.
Maybe in a dream, collective psychosis,
someone could come back
but prove it. You can't. You have to believe
ignorantly as in love, a cult equally awash
in imagination. Oneness comes
when you're most lost
like the souls illusioned in those photographs
or the body held back from the last edge
by the warm power of the other.

Meditation at the State Electric Café

An hour before the show and no home or warm
form to go to, only a low rumble of reggae
and voices echoing off the concrete floor:
a warehouse-coffeehouse where has-beens and
may-bes hang out between brainstorms. Writing
may help sometimes to dispel this strange full
emptiness, the whole horizon of sensations
you embrace which amount to nothing
even though a piano may suddenly sound
in the sternum and alert you to that ineffable
affirmation of the mundane, its beautifully plain
explosion of abstraction, a musing
over the everpresent vanishing
medicinal or merely healing hand
placed just so on the shoulder
or the smile of the small dark girl
slipping past your chair to join her sisters
as they sip cocoa with mom on the way home.

Your poems always vary on the same themes—
late-for-the-movie music when you can't decide
which picture you wish to see: flashes
of what already happened and you loved
or hated, or the immediate
unformed unfolding, uninformed
and out of uniform, the ink on the ribbons
fading in full sun, hanging over the back
of a chair in front of a window outside which
car steel banks angled daggers against glass
and glare bleaches out all old honors. It is
a chant or chance to relieve pain, the teenage
busgirl's gleaming profile entering the bloodstream
injectionlike, something rushing upward through taboo

to raise moral and immortal questions: When
does desire end? What battery does beauty perpetrate
so sweetly it destroys you without a touch? It's ancient
news, eternal in fact, at least as far back
as Sappho. My guitar case aches
with so many unplayed songs, its instrument
missing and the hollow creating a certain resonance
when you pass your hand over it like a paintbrush—
your hand, my hand, it's hard to be sure
in the shadows of these semitropical
trees in tubs which impose a certain rhythmic
piquancy, Afro-Cuban in origin, rhyming
with the clatter of coffee glasses and cash
registers chiming and espresso machines hissing
hot air not unlike his who pours himself out
pointlessly on a poorly lit little page.

But what can you do
when the room you sleep in is a dumping ground
for 40 years of high-school yearbooks
and a photo gallery of beefcake pinups
and mold is growing in the shower stall
and the dog in residence is a slavering wretch
shoving his wet nose into your crotch
or under your just-washed hand in search of affection.
The coffee jerks here serve soy cappuccino
and the customers sip to classic recorded jazz
and aerobic composers exercise the only way they know,
recording what comes along for consolation
across the street from the anarchist prep school
and the weekly *Expresso* whose inane reviews
prove journalism worthless in the wasted hands
of embezzlers destroyed by decades of cocaine.

Welcome home, soldier, remember the smoke
and blood you left on this battlefield
and are leaving still with every breath
you exhale? It reeks of reefer and seawater,
Jack Daniel's, popcorn, patchouli, garage fumes,
cigarette smoke and Chinese leftovers on your sleepless
fingers. You'd like to recline in a friendly embrace
and dissolve in pleasure and slumber, but
the table tilts and these trite desires
spill into oblivion where they belong.
Do you ever wonder why you undermine
your every utterance with its opposite—
a futile yet representative gesture
like the dance of the barechested boy on the skateboard
cutting figure-8s in the parking lot
by the lighthouse at midnight at the end of January
or the cruising gaze of the man your age
steering his Citroën along the cliffs
or the lone urinator in the public restroom
caught behind bars as the parks close.

David's Poem

Then I was a kid in the West Village
cruising the playgrounds in search of the best hoops
driving & dribbling & leaping for the shot
that swished thru the net in time
to Motown & Salsa & RocknRoll rhythms
backed by felafel frying
subways rumbling jazz rippling from the Vanguard late
espresso hissing & steaming
the hot sidewalk radiating waves of light
which bounced like a basketball off shimmering
blacktop

Now I'm alive to light in a new way
watching eyes or the sun's
angled glint off leaves in July
the sky winking shutterwise to catch
the exact glance of that girl in passing
that phantom vanishing as
light in its shadowy shifts
breaking downcourt like five fast guys
getting older & slower & slyer
in the flash of time

Later it's Spain & its white walls
Andalusian light washing the wild mind
of all time eternally the rocks washed
by sea spray which tosses up fine
reminders of original fire
singeing the aging soul
fathers discovered
ancestors unearthed by hand
brothers recovered in other tongues
& the warm wet tongues of lovers spicily
gathered & restored like old villagers'
rising reservoirs following summer storms

Carolyn's Invocation

As the sun climbs in the solstice sky
to warm the white page of inspiration

so too, Muse, come
& occupy the zone of most openness

in me, your faithless
lover, alive to everything but speechless

each sensation, each real understanding
unspeakable before the power of your

seduction, & so in silence, in hard
waiting, in the long stillness

before the fluid run of the blood
lights up the tired skull

hum your music thru my bluest mind
& find the song subtler than wind

sweeter than peaches fallen off a truck
which make a painting on the pavement

Artichoke Notes

You have to boil it the better part of an hour
after most of the day doing what should have been done
already in the windbroken bugeaten garden but at least
it was warm for once with a fat moon brewing
unseen but bound to come up and water flowing
calmly through the hose into the roses' roots and gopher holes
and freshly whacked bolted endive topping the compost

so the pitiful little plants were given a drink
and dry straw tucked in all around their beds
mulching the weeds down and the water in and
giving the gardener some small illusion
of control as slugs and other predators plot
and the cat lies fat in the shade oblivious
to the conspiracy of marauding rodents

the last of the lettuces are slightly embittered
but better than what you can buy and as you wait
for the next course boiling away on the stove
you read insane and strangely compelling stories
of backstage fiascos and murder-suicides and book reviews
by classicists accurately calling doom by its other names
farms dying memory betraying its losses all the escaping
and perishing sweetness imagined for a minute flashing before

like the face in the grocery store introduced just
as the line was moving through the checkout chute
and you were torn from that hint of unity
or the call you missed because you weren't home
and tape stretches only so far or the dance
at the VFW hall where all the kids in town
are twisting even now as you peel
each leaf at last in search of the heart's
elusive taste so tender
so much effort and
it's gone

Samba from the Portuguese

Permission is requested to speak Brazilian
a sex-stricken Romance language
one more lexicon with which to indulge
a certain abandoned sadness
which translates happily into a celebration
of the capacity to endure desolation
how paradoxical & hardly even
poetic but true
a samba of sad gratitude
a scat which passes for Joycean gibberish
without the heaviness or resonance of history
just a here-&-now sort of ordinary misery
secular & pedestrian
which walks with a certain bossa nova beat
swiveling subtly about the hips
like an Egyptian princess
or an Italian torch singer
impersonating Pasolini & gasoline

Modigliani's Garage Sale

My stuff is spread out on the sidewalk
in the sun of a Saturday afternoon
because I'm moving, my lover left, I got evicted,
lost my job and I need the cash
that might be dropped from a passing car.
The smell of tacos from the taquería next door
blends with the cheesy aroma snaking around the corner
from the cheese shop and the electric spark
of the streetcar on Carl Street,
passengers squinting behind the smoked glass
headed for all manner of meetings
and missed connections, traffic
across the bridge into the tranquil suburbs a slow crawl
punctuated after all by honeysuckle
near an outdoor café table
where the cruelest of beautiful birdsongs
torments Modigliani awaiting his elusive model
who he intuits may have consigned him to the monastic artistry
of the painter left brushless at the end of a long day
when strangers have come and cleaned out his garage.
He counts the take as the clock whispers oblivion
and images of her missing face
refuse to appear in the shopwindows,
consummate portrait of the unattainable.

Metroplitan Afterlife

The chamber ensemble hammers & saws
in the Great Hall at cocktail hour
where after an afternoon in Beauty's thrall
Chinese jades & porcelain plates competing
with eternal passing faces
I'm taking shelter from a spring shower
sipping an ancient drink

why should the sight of art make the heart hurt
as if struck hard in the chest by beloved fists
& why the undying desire to possess

the marble rumbles with the murmur of culture hunters
& the fixed Egyptians just upstairs from the restrooms
witness mutely their enduring fate
displayed amid the flow of transient
flesh which gathers lingering in the gift shops

a few blocks away the tchotchkes of the deceased
are auctioned off for astronomical sums
so in the comfort of their own museums
collectors may feel Celebrity's side effects
which last as long as magazines remember

on silk scrolls
in ceramic bowls
in fragments of carved stone
in oils & pigments slathered on canvas
in cast bronze tortured into surrendering shapes
in vibrating violin strings
the visions shimmer
mirages & miracles of the real

"See you could spend from 9 o'clock
in the morning until now here
& you still wouldn't see the whole place"

Allen Ginsberg Aloft

It's only fit you should die in April
National Poetry Month
the foolish month
so many flowers spewing their perfume
wherever the wind might twist
immortal spring of your flare in the evening sky
the final trace of your fame a cockeyed grin
flashing across the cosmos
you were the one who should have stood
bald & bearded at the Capitol
some frosty January afternoon
chanting a sutra for the new President
ah but you were too queer too radical
Jewish-anarchist-pacifist-Buddhist-
existential-transcendentalist
disabused of illusions
drug experienced & wildly traveled
to every corner of consciousness
promiscuously alive
at home in your own mind
in any country where a bard was called for
ready to compose in a moment
like a fairy gunfighter godfather
armed with quickdraw rollerball
& backup pens in your pocket protector
taking dictation from the angels
yet never a-scared to dance with the demons too
nothing personal just pure spirit
breathing its song thru your incorrigible
incorruptible inexhaustible loco-
motivated soul your sun-
flower supermarket no apologies
vastly ambitious selflessly self-centered

unwhimpering bang-up end-of-the-millennium
vision open to embrace whatever
came
you've come along all my writing life
to the last leaves of this little book
of lists & first drafts
learned from your example
the habit of noting what happens
FLYING EAGLE MADE IN CHINA

stamped on the back page
ironic bird for a "four-eyed sissy"
still it intimates where you've soared
over all States all Walls
roaring the whole truth & all the news unfit
all words & deeds & moods & foolishness
allowed in the big archival collective
inclusion you gathered & let go
with every prodigal ancient postfuturist
breath you blew thru your brave lungs
into the air
we live & breathe
& the tears
we taste of your greatness

Visitations

I knew them when they were alive
and now they're gone
these men whose photographs
haunt my house
as if it were a museum
or mausoleum of the missing
presences felt and lost
and recovered only in ghostly
visitations
like Blake at Ginsberg's window
or Allen at various ages
clipped from newspapers
gazing resolutely from nowhere
over my desk
Henry waving Julio brooding
Bukowski subtly grinning
Neruda gloomily musing
Rexroth beaming in Japanese
García Lorca whispering Andalusian
can I begin to justify their company
will I accomplish the demanded task
should I presume
to use the languages
they mastered before I started
and what does this add
how many words does the world need

Written in the Kitchen at Terry & Carolyn's

Overripe apricots drop to the sidewalk
exuding perfume of 1954
the tree outside our kitchen window then
the same summer Mom lost control of the Olds
and totalled it against a telephone pole
on Airport Boulevard
so long ago

today July light is dappling the table
with ripe reminders of lives and ideas
rescued by scholars patiently plying libraries
milking the memories and memoirs of survivors
alive just long enough to spill what they've witnessed
the bodies buried or embraced
the mouths whose words or kisses were historic
the hands that shut the gas off
after the quake

homes fall apart and are fixed
and decay again but not before
rambling troubadours stay a few days
to feed the fish and medicate the cat
and float lightly among the silent books
and pluck with alacrity the clattering keys
of the portable Underwood
which needs cleaning

and not before farmers have hauled their crops
all green and golden to the parking lots
merchants alarmed by the bare arms of girls
offering the fruits of their youth the ripe reds
and purples of peaches and plums and the breads

as brown as the sellers' baked faces
gracious sunlight pouring its gourmet organic
dressing over everything

everything spilling richly some of it caught
some escaping the net of quick ink
woven to record what can't be bought
or taught to rhyme with police car sirens
speeding down Cedar Street in pursuit
of panhandlers shoplifters promiscuous minstrels
while behind blushing Victorian walls
a transient Romantic revels in the bruised aura
of fallen apricots and savors
what is revealed

Pastoral

Daryl in tight jeans & cutoff t-shirt,
tattoos on his tanned arms,
white mime gloves hugging his expressive hands,
guides my car into the oil-change bay
and I walk a hundred yards to a green park
on the outskirts of Santa Rosa
to sit under redwood shade and read,
content with the temperature,
the blazing grass rich enough to lie down in,
the undulating hills probably built by bulldozers,
even the shell of an old Corvair
like a parking-lot Giacometti
& last night's condom
left in the gutter on Todd Road.
The sky over this oasis
ignores the warehouses & adjacent workshops
or re-creates them in its own radiance
as sculptures even lovelier than the gutted Chevy—
shapes made to pulsate, corrugated, in cerulean light
cooled by the jade of great trees.
It seems as if the freeway down the street
will never again smell of ripped steel & scorched
flayed rubber and no flares will need to be set
by men in uniforms, red lights twisting
atop their cruisers, and no ambulance will arrive
because a day this perfect can hurt no one.

Vallejo Remembers

Do you still make that little buzzing sound
between your teeth as your lover is coming?
you were the only woman I ever knew
who did that
and it was immensely sexy
20 years ago?
or whenever it was we were given our time together
and here comes the sound of the cable-car cable
heard from your bed
as it hummed and clanked under Mason Street
and the tall glass of water you always placed on the nightstand
and your fluffy white terrycloth robe and the down comforter
and your mandolin or was it a balalaika?
and when I lay behind you cradling your little breasts
you'd grind your butt so deliciously into my belly
those nights on Russian Hill
just up from Keystone Korner and the police station
on a street named after a Peruvian poet
still reach me sometimes when I'm in the neighborhood
on the border between the smells of the Chinese fish markets
and the erotic garlicky aromas of the Italian restaurants
red wine running through our brains and tongues
there was something radiant about those hours
so what if you made a habit of being late
it's so much later now
what matters is what endures of our connection
brief as it was
a certain indelible residue
of tenderness

Retrospective Sketch

The floor was sloped
so the studio door swung open
because the tongue of the lock
was always slipping out of the slot
with a long slow squeak
as the hinges pivoted
and the smell of oils and solvents
those artistic toxics
seductive as musk
came floating out of cool darkness
to envelop us as we lay
in our bed by the fireplace
entwined for a while
in the late spring of our lives
creators of daily legends
twinned in thickening strands
like a French braid
handsomely sweeping the rich hair
away from your face
your Botticelli cheekbones
revealed like the charcoal sketch
you'd make on one of your stretched
and gessoed canvases
before you'd begin to paint
stoned in that room with the sloped floor
whose door swung open sometimes
as we mated

F. Scott Fitzgerald Meets the Wolf Man

A moonless night, but anything might happen
over a long letter that exceeds an ounce
and contains unconsciously occult allusions
to drawers full of gorgeous shirts
out of which silver chest hairs sprout
and which a slim woman may covet and carry away
to drape on her own bones, heedless
of their feral interior.
How my closet aches for that skeleton,
her lithe, cool body, nimble mind
reading a book in my bed
while the stars display themselves promiscuously
like those excessive lights spread out across L.A.
seen from the hills above the HOLLYWOOD sign.
Ever notice how a werewolf moans
as he's transformed, or roars when he comes,
as I do in her arms, ferociously in love
nine years on, despite having been cured.
Like falling off a bike, you never forget how.
Or rolling at exhilarating speed down a steep road
hoping you hit no bump or dip
that flings you fatally against a tree.
Elegant sentences do not suffice,
nor do those famous rides
in taxicabs' backseats when New York is yours
because your novel is hot and your lover's thigh
is pressed to excite and tenderize your night.
Such savory moments are quickly spent
like bittersweet chocolate melting on the tongue,
which turns for consolation to paper and pen
and the taste of glue on the backs of stamps.

The Dead of Winter

Time and chance happen to everyone.
Death is not news, but in case of fame
headlines sprout through the snow.
Comedians don't know quite what to say.
Month before last it might have been me,
facing the wrong way in the fast lane,
my powerful car crippled beside the guardrail.
Somehow I stood unscathed in the darkening rain
to wait for the flashing lights and dazzling black eyes
of the handsomest highway patrolman I've ever seen.
A scientist named Seed contends he will be God
by making sterile people parents of clones.
How can fiction proceed under such premises.
Where would they find the names.
Every dreamed-up thing has been pre-abused.
Trees have intervened with the force of trains—
unyielding, not to be hugged, at least on skis.
Speed may kill, but slowness can also maim,
as in those poems that brood on gloom and go nowhere,
hoping in vain to hatch some hopeful chirp
or song that might take flight, some sign of life.
Like that chaotic flock
careening through the sky this afternoon
just as the rain began, randomness
scattering happily, or so it looked—bright
in the heart of so much darkness—flying sparks.
Up in the newsrooms reporters stare into screens,
fingers sprinting over the plastic keys.
Backstage, writers of the late-night monologues
type the jokes fast, racing against deadlines.

Tourists at Birkenau

While Sean stood watch
for patrolling guards
Eduardo clipped
a quick bit of wire
rusty barbed witness

& picked up shards
of plates by the tracks
where herded passengers
last disembarked

later he placed them
in a cigar tin
oxidized metal
& ceramic chip
resting strangely
on blue-black velvet

some sort of artifact
pieces of evidence
charged with oblivion
only the living
can ever remember

In Absence of Bootstraps

Pulling my socks on this morning
my lower back snapped
and suddenly I was old, walking stooped
like my father returning home tired from the track.
At my age he'd made millions behind a desk,
negotiating over the phone, traveling on planes
through long skies to hours-away outposts
of the marketplace, and his stride showed pain,
his moves getting up from his chair
to change the football game
effortful like those of an old fullback
tackled too many times.
At the end, atop a mountain of privileged offspring,
peering into the promised land of relief,
he understood what he'd paid to make ease possible—
or if not ease, a certain tenuous shelter
constructed all his life, wrecking his back.
It must have seemed strange, some kind of joke,
that life's work, leaving it all
to a scattering band of descendants
to gamble beyond his most meticulous plans.
The curse of purposeless toil, absurd, save to provide
and thus make possible various lives
including mine, whose poetry I owe
to a fellowship I'll never be sure I earned.
Pulling my socks up I snap
because I have no bootstraps,
no struggle beyond the impossible one
with words, which fail
again   and again   and again

Typing with Mr. Moss

The most important class I took in high school was typing.
Mr. Moss was a dork with a nervous tic but that chart
at the front of the room showing where the letters were
on the keyboard taught me to train my fingers,
one useful skill acquired at that miserable institution.
Lots of the smart kids got very successful, more or less
running the world now, and even some of the underachievers
are making fortunes as entrepreneurs, in the professions,
in entertainment or at the top of horrible corporations.
I'm one of those who didn't do so well, then
or now, still more or less content to loaf and invite
cats, raptors, dragonflies, maybe wash the kitchen floor
every few months as needed, water the vegetables, whack
back weeds and neglect the perennials, which are parched.
In a few days my lover will arrive mysteriously
for a while before disappearing
again, and I understand this is necessary,
a recurrent condition, like yardwork or housekeeping:
Every season you need to split more kindling.
No matter how clean you sweep it there's always more dust.
There's also a light breeze and green shadows
and bright-colored butterflies which sometimes
when you're hurtling along the ridge road
float smack into the grill of your pickup.
And then there's this other, less lethal
streamlined instrument of precise steel
and cream-gray plastic casing, classical as any piano
Leonard Bernstein banged on as a way of seducing his students.
Maybe Mr. Moss was a closet case, that's why he was so
jittery, or he just couldn't believe he was stranded
in Business Education teaching twerps like me
and adolescent delinquents too dumb or distracted
even to learn to type. I learned
more or less, but to what end it is unclear.

Bad Mood

I bark at the telemarketer
because I'm tired of too many choices,
tired of trying to keep track of what I owe
to whom & for how long, tired of trying to save money
by wasting time switching from one deal to another,
& when the phone rings I want it to be a friend,
not some automaton reading my name off a screen.
I'm sick of the newspapers I'm addicted to,
sick of the book reviews, the weeklies, the quarterlies,
sick of information & advertising, sick of opinions,
sick of literature & sick of my own ignorance.
& let's not forget the rain
which I've had up to here but it keeps falling
halfway thru May while the tomatoes pray
for a little heat & the woodpile shrinks
& wilts & I keep feeling the need to ask
permission to exist because how have I earned the right
& why have I done so little with the chance.
Happiness hurts so I prefer suffering,
it seems so truly human & I long to identify
with people I can't relate to otherwise.
I want to strike up a conversation
with strangers in the supermarket but it's always
freezing in there & I have a long list,
the fish are glittering in their icy case
but I know they've been stolen from the ocean
where they belong & let's not even mention meat.
What can I say or eat to compensate
for what I consume—I could survive on as little
as a little lettuce, like Simon of the Desert,
but instead I spend hours brewing elaborate soups
& sipping them deliciously & a little guiltily
& reading *The New York Times* & listening to the news

which I know by heart like an album of old folk songs.
& when the phone rings it's only because some company
wants my account & that's why I cut off the pitch
& unleash a streak of abuse to illustrate
why this kid should find some other job
& why I want instead to receive a call
from someone I'd want to meet for a meal in town
or invite over here to share what I've made
while it rains.

Election Night

My ballot dutifully stabbed, I am a citizen.
With shopping, 5-speed transmission, child support,
an orange cat whose hairs appear everywhere
like the single long blond strand I found in the car
from who knows what unfathomable head.
One shoulder lamb chop, trimmed, cubed, seared
and slowly stewed with vegetables and news.
One aching sunset through cool clouds.
The one Republican who uses pot
defeated.   Therefore I decline to smoke.
No drug can make whole what sentiment has wrecked.
And one must honor pain, which arrives in time to remind.
Don't interrupt. Don't contradict. Don't ask.
The system works. Feel how blood just moves.
If something malfunctions you can take a pill.
All the governors are alive and gray. Radios say so.
And of course guns. Every child must tote one. I did.
Then I ran for president and won, like JFK, proving
I too was popular that year. Now I'd like to be liked
but for new reasons. Not for my personality but being
really bad, bad enough to say what can't be thought.
Slamming the obsolete keys to release a bittersweet sound,
the kind of music a masseuse would understand.
That focused therapeutic stroke along troubled muscle.
Sinew renewed through the truth of touch.
The body all but beyond politics.

Chaos Theory

Hitler thought the stars were made of ice.
Sometimes astronauts drop their screwdrivers,
which orbit Earth until puncturing spacecraft.
SWAT teams do not administer CAT scans.
Ogden Nash and Dr. Seuss
never appeared on the same stage.
What in the sky rhymes with time?
Answer: a herd of clouds.
Showering outdoors in early winter
one feels invigorated, temperate, elect,
whatever calamaties are occurring elsewhere—
proof this world is probably the best.
Do the math.
It all adds up. Saul Bellow said so.
One is born under a deadline with no outline.
You open the blank blue book for the final and let fly.
What can be told alone in elliptic loops
ordinary prose obscures. Logic is like
a backhoe violating nature with a straight line
in which to lay pipe for plumbing.
Freely one fails to detail
a full accounting of experience.
The mere thought of it turns you vertiginous.
The words come back stamped insufficient.
What string stroked by which bow
resonates in Sinatra when some snotnosed
mafioso is stomped in a parking lot
in darkest Vegas
and no policeman or comedian
appears to stanch nor even hand
a hanky to snivel into?
This is the whole cloth and nothing but,
a form of crime and confession at the same time,

only without the law—
except for those blinding lights by the roadside,
the same scary cruiser that comes to the rescue
after you've failed to arrive,
your career a skid.
Whose voice is that? Oh, just a late poet
on the radio, taped ages ago, now resurrected
and echoing spookily. There goes
the old vain pain of losing the youthful looks.
And look at this: the large dog
suddenly takes a bite of the child's face.
Everything that falls erodes the road down,
its ruts arrested for a spell by blue shale
over which we roll
slowly
moving out toward mail.
You want to know so what.
I can't say except to sob,
muffled by retort before I start, doubtful
whatever I report
will make the cut. Mushroom poachers
skulk through the woods toting plastic bags.
Supermarket clerks decode *The New York Times*,
sounding those little beeps, 7 cents tax.
One might as well surf naked
carrying a torch at midnight under a full moon
and be seen only by lonesome werewolves
or startled cosmonauts dropping their violins,
which is that strange sound
you may hear circling,
something like the great discoverers
crashing lost into blind lands
to which they gave wrong names in ignorance.
Know what I mean?
You drive like that
and they take your license away,

leaving only a noise of noxious revving
to *wha-wha* in some garage.
Remove gravity and men drift on wind.
Warning to mice: you may ignite if you bite wire.
Above traffic, trees can be heard trembling.
Cricket-gossip, coughing frogs, doomed moths rattling lampshades
and hungry skunks on front porches rummaging through kindling
make wild music amid tall thickets
of randomly blooming volunteer arugula.
It doesn't take a rocket scientist.

Having a Smoke with the Buddha

After the plate of pasta with chopped tomatoes—
a variation on the recipe
that Carmen introduced me to
before she died—
I step outside as the moon rises
and strike a kitchen match against the Buddha's bald head
to light my cigarette on the back porch
and watch night start
in what seems at last to be summer.
He's made of concrete, and around his neck
is draped a foot of heavy rusted chain,
its ends linked over his belly by a weathered padlock:
MASTER, the lock declares, and the Buddha is laughing.
As I smoke in the peaceful dusk I think of the owl
Kate's neighbor saw over by the river
carrying off what looked like a skunk,
clumps of black & white fur
scattered on the ground, unlucky animal
fighting to the end against a superior power.
Later, more bits of fur and a skull were found.
The slow moon climbs, round and luminous
as the floodlight on a police car.
Miles of bluish fog cruise just offshore
above the muffled rumble of rolling surf.
The tobacco burns
between drags which bring me
that rapturous deathlike rush
of calming yet rapacious intoxication.
The Buddha, cool and gray, tougher than weather,
invites me to be like him, good-natured, impervious,
happily bearing the weight of his chain, his lock,
his place on the rail with his back to the west.
But I'm not. I am flesh and breath,
which add up to something less.

Deep Song

When the sea floor
drops off
into sudden darkness
the swimmer at the surface
feels its shifting depth

as when in flamenco
the singer's voice
plunges off a cliff
into pure loss

which turns to a fearful soaring
shot through with gorgeous suffering
tremulously adept
like hummingbird maneuvers around a hot bloom
red in the light of a July afternoon

whose heat has given birth
to turning youth
ripening
into a deeper
beauty
alive to the sorrows of understanding

beyond promise
just past optimism and
grazing the far side of every
consolation

save love

which holds
and deepens
across impossible distances
touching unspeakably
its bound souls

and won't let go

Movers

The dancer the acrobat the athlete the pedestrian
appear to be moving from where I sit
sculpting space with gratuitous beauty
like dolphins like dragonflies like pumas
like people
proving themselves alive
under a night's rain
or a day's layered clarity and clouds
steeplechasing over woodpiles
turning double plays
flipping through space like ospreys
my visions above the rivermouth

and of course and always
cacophonous steel violating twilight
on wheels turned by routine
even as ravens survey streams of taillights
cruising for abandoned cadavers
the paramedics have overlooked
near the left turn into the last landfill

what I don't know hurts me
all those accusatory spines
lettered with revelations I'll never caress
while gazing into their pages
the paintings I fail to ogle in the closed galleries
the poets whose farewell readings
I leave town to miss
this mortal ignorance aches
like a mailbox for envelopes yet to arrive
my love's report on her new life
the check confirming my official success

percussive recipes are drummed into roofs
as if to compete with the late news
always the same somehow
same news same rain
same gusts blown through night
to no apparent end
traces of light unseen above the storm

are tears tiny explosions
are lovers bombers in pursuit of suicide
or merely driven to move like commuters
through dangerous everyday necessity
swerving to avoid spilled
unidentified fluids
which might be rivers in another world

beautiful rivers where birds dive
and light glints upward
into a bright sky

Guitars of the Diaspora

A flock of motorcycles
is flashing swiftly past freshly split fenceposts
along a road near the ocean
where an osprey glides
over a warm shoreline in late April
after an endless and relentless winter
when slopes were mudflows
and roads were sucked into sinkholes
and homes were pitched face-first into the surf

just what the world needs
swimmers without wetsuits diving into waves
and 80-degree days when lovely girls
in bikinis parade on Beach Street
relieving and increasing the bittersweet misery
welling up in solitary men

former sweethearts stand in parking structures
breathing the noxious fumes as they kiss goodbye
wistfully anticipating time
envisioning freeways along which they're fated
to drive forever with no sign of relief

only the guitars of the diaspora
ghostly fiddlers from condemned barracks
whose plangent melodies echo for decades
evoking nightmares and a strange nostalgia
none but the ancient sages might decipher

just what the world needs
street musicians repeating
the same eternal songs in perpetuity

Stephen Kessler was born in 1947 in Los Angeles. He is the author of five previous books and chapbooks of original poetry and the translator of nine books of poetry and fiction from Spanish, including works by Fernando Alegría, Julio Cortázar, Pablo Neruda, Ariel Dorfman, and Nobel laureate Vicente Aleixandre. His essays, criticism and journalism have appeared widely in the independent literary and alternative press since the early 1970s. He was a founding editor and publisher of small poetry presses Green Horse Press and Alcatraz Editions, the international journal *Alcatraz*, and weekly newspapers the *Santa Cruz Express* and *The Sun*. Later he edited *OutLook*, a Mendocino County monthly. He makes his home on the coast of Northern California, where he edits *The Redwood Coast Review*.